TITO
The Frito Bandito

TITO
The Frito Bandito

Marie Weldon

authorHOUSE®

AuthorHouse™
1663 Liberty Drive
Bloomington, IN 47403
www.authorhouse.com
Phone: 1-800-839-8640

First published by AuthorHouse   10/14/2011

ISBN: 978-1-4670-6069-1 (sc)
ISBN: 978-1-4670-6068-4 (ebk)

Library of Congress Control Number: 2011918113

Printed in the United States of America

Any people depicted in stock imagery provided by Thinkstock are models, and such images are being used for illustrative purposes only.
Certain stock imagery © Thinkstock.

This book is printed on acid-free paper.

Contents

This book is dedicated to my daughter,

Dorothy Murray,

an accomplished horsewoman, trainer, breeder, showman
and promoter of the Arabian horse.

It is my hope that the readers of my books will enjoy the
stories and learn proper care and handling of animals in
general, love and compassion for them, to know that
they are totally dependent on us for all their needs, how
important a schedule is for them as it is for us, that they
expect to be fed at the same time each day and to have fresh
water available all the time.

A New Home

As I look back over my life I realize it has been good; that I have been loved and well cared for, have had many good friends and families that I enjoyed working with as well as helping many children learn to love, appreciate and care for animals.

It was a fall day when visitors came to our ranch; the rains had already started on the west side of the Cascades in this small Oregon town. My rider had outgrown me and was training on her new larger horse, leaving me with little to do. This was worrisome, not knowing what was going to happen to me. My mother always told me to be a good pony and good things would come to me. That is a tall order for ponies as many are left with children who do not know how to take care of them or handle them, who unknowingly hurt us trying to communicate what they want us to do, having no instruction and often their parents are uneducated to the needs of a horse, or how to handle them as well. Due to our size we seldom receive professional training like larger horses but instead we are given to children as a pet. Seldom are we in the hands of a child with knowledgeable adult supervision that participates in the handling and training period of our lives. Many ponies are said to be mean, nasty little horses because they get tired of this kind of treatment and fight back with bites and throwing their riders. This gives all of us a bad name, but we can take only so much abuse before we must save ourselves. You have all heard the story of the pony that threw someone when they were a child so now they have no use for ponies and many do not have anything to do with horses because of this.

I was one of the lucky ones with a great family. I had special training for my little rider who was deaf, so I had to be the ears for both of us and what was around us. I had to be especially sensitive to my riders every move and watch for things for her safety. We did a lot of trail riding in the mountains and rode in some of the greatest parades ever.

We participated in the very prestigious Portland Rose Festival Parade. It was 5 miles long, took hours to complete, crossing open bridges over the Willamette River, winding up and down the Portland streets, through the crowds of thousands. Kids would run out to touch us and pet us as we went by. There was lots of noise from the fire trucks in the parade and people announcing each entry as it passed by and what it had won. We waited for hours before the Parade started and hours after it was over for traffic to thin out so we could go home. There was all the cleaning and checking of the equipment before we entered the line because you would not have anything with you to fix something if it broke. We always had sacks of candy to carry to throw to the kids along the way.

These visitors daughter "Dottie" was three; about the same age my present owner was when I was first trained for her. This girl also had special needs in a horse as she wore leg braces to correct her crooked way of walking. Her horse would have to be very careful not to get tangled in the braces as she moved around him. I heard them say they had Arabian horses but they wanted a horse Dottie's size for her to train with, a horse she could learn to halter, brush, saddle and bridle all by herself, a size she could get on without a mounting block and ride when ever she liked, not having to depend on her mom or dad to help her. She had no fear she had been riding for as long as she could set up. She received her first trophy at 11 months and often sat on Tiger, their Arabian stallion as he waited for a class Dottie's mother was riding in. She had grown up at horse shows with Tiger nuzzling her as she laid in the overhead boot of the horse truck Dottie's parents used to go to the shows in. There was a mattress up there so if they had to stay overnight they had a place to sleep and Dottie had a place to take a nap when she became too tired during the show.

Dottie's mom was a professional trainer and was building a training stable and breeding farm of beautiful Arabian horses. The family enjoyed trail riding when they were not showing and they had a 4-H club that performed at fairs and in parades. They talked about getting me when my present rider was confident in her new horse and no longer needed me. It was settled I would move in the spring to their farm. I was feeling good that I would be going to a home of knowledgeable horse people, pretty sure there would be no bad feed or treatment coming my way.

It was exciting to think of larger pastures and more horses to run with and get acquainted with. I would get to go out more with this family and see different places and meet many new friends, maybe even some my own size. The one thing most of use miss in our lives is friends our own size. Seems seldom that folks have more than one pony for some reason they only seem to need one of us at a time. Dottie has a little brother; maybe they will get him a pony too one can only hope. They seem to favor girls around here, that would be nice.

Pasture Pals

Spring came and with it Dottie's parents and the truck. They did not live far and I would get to see my old owners when we all went trail riding together. They all belonged to the same Parade and Trail riding club so often went out together for a weekend get together. That is how they knew I would be available for sale as soon as my rider changed to a larger horse. It was a larger ranch with many pastures and more horses. There was Tiger a beautiful bay Arabian stallion, Muz a beautiful bay Arabian mare and Gypsy a tall leggy bay Anglo Arabian mare. They were all show horses. Gypsy had been retired as Dottie's fathers trail horse; he did not ride much his job kept him away from home a lot. Often there would be other horses at the ranch, in training or being boarded there. Once a week there would be a 4-H meeting in the big outdoor arena with all the kids and their horses practicing for a show or parade. There were lessons being given so lots more excitement than I had seen before. I made many new friends, learned their names and enjoyed our weekly gatherings. There were two other ponies in the club, so finally someone I did not have to look up at.

Most Arabians have nicknames because their real name or registered name is usually strangely spelled, long and very hard to pronounce. Tiger's registered name was Tagiz,

Muz was Missafir and Gypsy was Gypsy Arabia Kyram. You can see why they had nick names; it would be hard to call them by some of these names when you wanted them to come in out of the pasture. There was one Arabian mare in training whose name was Kris. This was very unusual for an Arabian name to be so plain and short. At one show the ring steward went down the line getting the horses names for the announcer so he would pronounce then correctly when the placing was called. When he came to Kris he said "just plain Kris?" Yes Dottie's mother said. When they called Chris's placing in the class the announcer said "and third place goes to just plain Kris". Everyone laughed and her owners were very surprised.

I was not turned out in the pasture but kept in the yard on a tether line around the house most of the time so Dottie could visit anytime she liked. I had to be very careful not to get her caught in the tether line when walking up to her. Her mother gave her instruction on how to properly clean my feet, brush my coat and feed me. She would saddle and bridle me and give us lessons in the big outdoor arena. Making sure Dottie learned to warm me up and ask me to move and change gaits with lots of instruction on keeping her hands quiet so not to jerk my mouth. She taught everyone to warm the bit when it was cold in their hands before putting it into our mouths so the cold steel would not stick to our tongue in the winter. She taught bit washing after every ride so it would be clean for the next use. This reduces the chance of spreading decease when a bit is used on more than one horse. As I became acquainted with the rest of the horses I was allowed out in the big pasture each day after lessons. Gypsy and I became friends; she was Dottie's mom's first horse. She knew lots of tricks and often performed for visitors and friends who came to the ranch. Gypsy said, "We have a great owner, you will never be mistreated or underfed here". I was bathed, clipped, feet trimmed every six weeks, and we had yearly vet checks. I was vaccinated; my teeth floated (if needed) to make sure I was healthy and could eat properly.

As summer emerged and the rains stopped construction started on a new barn. It was huge. I had never seen a barn this big. It had an indoor arena with big stalls around three sides; there would be no riding in the rain this winter. I had my own stall, bedded deep in shavings with an automatic waterier and fresh eastern Oregon alfalfa fed twice daily with our grain and vitamins. Ten of the stalls had long turn out pens attached so we could exercise and visit with our neighbors on either side. We could also visit with the horses in the big pasture at the end of the turnouts. It was great. The family was very protective of my small size and made sure the new horses coming and going couldn't hurt me with their playful kicks and running in the field. I only went out to the big field with Muz and Gypsy. They were my best friends and very careful not to run into me or kick me when they were playing around.

A big new horse came to the ranch. Her name was Behold, and she was a Thoroughbred racehorse that had been injured on the race track. She was purchased by the equestrian center where Dottie's mom worked for a school horse. She was to be trained to jump but could not due to her old race track injuries. She did not tolerate being stalled all the time and started throwing her students and then running wildly around the arena until someone caught her. Wendy, the English instructor asked the director of the school to sell Behold now that she was "uncontrollable." This meant she could be sold for slaughter. When Dottie's mom heard this she quickly went to the director and asked what price he wanted for Behold, "$650" he said. Dottie's mom purchased her and brought her home. We needed another school horse and she would not be locked in a stall all the time. She would be out in the pasture so she could work off the energy she had that caused her to act up when penned up all the time.

Dottie's mom worked the race track in her early days and knew racehorses liked a stall companion when they were locked up all the time. I became that companion and we had our own pasture fenced just for us. This meant we went to pasture everyday except when we had lessons. It was great because I got to ride every lesson with Behold to comfort her. Only advanced riders were allowed on her to make sure she was not hurt, scared or wrongly handled. Behold was a great lesson horse now that she was not locked in a stall all the time, and was my best buddy. We would play tricks on Dottie when she came into the pasture to catch me.

I was the only horse allowed to wear my halter in the pasture just so Dottie could catch me. Halters are not left on the larger horses because it is easy for them to catch on a steel fence post if they scratch their heads. If they panic and fight they have been known to choke to death or break their necks trying to get away. If the halter is too loose they can get their foot in it and break their leg trying to get untangled. For these reasons a horse should never be turned out to pasture with a halter on. If they must wear a halter then it needs to fit properly and be checked every day so it does not wear sores on our face when we eat.

I would run around and around Behold when Dottie was trying to catch me and when she was just close enough to grab me I would duck under Behold's belly to the other side. Behold was just tall enough for me to go under her belly just touching my back as I passed under. This worked great until one day Dottie ducked under Behold behind me and grabbed my halter. We thought it was harmless fun but Dottie's mom scolded me because I had put Dottie in harms way causing her to be that close to a big horse in an uncontrolled situation. Had Behold moved, Dottie could have been hurt and it would have been my fault. I was trained to protect her not put her in harms way. Behold had a bad reputation with people giving Dottie's mom good reason to be leery of this situation. I was separated from Behold and put back in a stall with its own paddock where I could not play this game with her again.

I was not the only horse in the barn. There was Jill a Morab (half Morgan, half Arabian). She belonged to the Eaton's who also owned Kris, one of the Arabians in training. Jill had also been at the equestrian center as a school horse. The center was closing and the student that always rode Jill would be taking lessons at our house from now on. Muz and Gypsy were also used as school horses at our house.

Behold worked that summer for us and was purchased by a student who loved her. It had to be a good home or Dottie's mom would not have sold her. Dottie's mom always looked after us when we were going to new homes. She made an open offer to take us back if anything did not work or they could not keep us for any reason. It was a great comfort to know that we would only go to homes of great care and know that we were coming back if that home did not work out.

I went back to the pasture with Muz and Gypsy when I was not in my own paddock and stall area. Dottie's mother did not have to worry about them hurting her. She had trained both of them and knew exactly what they would do. Neither one of them was tall enough for me to walk under anyway, nor would they have put up with it.

Lessons

Dottie had grown up with horses nuzzling her and taking her for short rides when her mother had a minute between lessons. She was eager to have her own horse to ride; one she could saddle and bridle all by herself. Then she could ride anytime she wanted too without bothering her mom or dad to get her horse ready.

Dottie had mastered grooming and putting on the saddle and bridle. I would put my head in the bridle and open my mouth so she could slide the bit in between my teeth. We had several lessons a week and Dottie was getting rather good with her riding. It was common for Dottie to have me saddled and riding in the big arena as soon as horses were fed and breakfast was over. She had not mastered getting me to lope, so she would trot me as fast as I could go around the arena laughing all the way. I was also trained to pull a cart. Dottie also received instruction on driving me. Dottie was not big enough to harness me and too young to understand the importance of how to hitch me to the cart. Therefore she only was able to drive when her mother had time to harness and hitch me up. This was great because now her little brother Art could enjoy the fun and ride in the cart with her. He did not seem to like horses as much as she did. He would rather play on the tractor and watch as others rode.

We had worked hard with lessons and 4-H meetings, but Dottie was not old enough to be in 4-H. We went to the 4-H shows but she could only watch and I was not allowed to go. The Club had 6 matched chestnut Arabian horses and started a parade team. Dottie's mom would dress in old Cowboy attire and ride Tiger in the Western working class. Dottie would ride me in the youngest riders division. I would follow Tiger down the street and he would follow the 4-Hers so Dottie's mom could supervise the team. We were winning trophies right and left. We were even invited to Grand Marshal a parade in Washington State. It was great. We would eat donuts while waiting for the parades to start and snack on Frito's when the parade was over. I love Fritos. I would poke around in lunch sacks to find open bags and flip my head up and down to dump them out so I could eat them. So came the name Frito Bandito. I could smell them a mile away and knew every trick to get them out of the bag. The 4-Hers learned early on to guard their lunches if they had Fritos in them, I even figured out how to put my foot on the bag and tear it open if it hadn't already been opened.

One thing that made lessons so great was the games we played. This would help the rider relax and enjoy riding while they were really working to learn something new. One of the games was to ride bare back with a dollar under the rider's knee. The last rider with the dollar won all the dollars from everyone else. Then there was sitting in a chair with a kick ball between their knees to strengthen their legs to grip the horse with their thigh. The rider uses their thigh to stay on us and their lower leg to cue us what to do. They would have contests to see whose grip was the best by sitting looking at each other and squeezing each other's knees. One was squeezing the other pushing to keep them from getting your knees together. This is a great exercise to help you stay on your horse and still have your lower leg loose to cue with. We would have trotting matches to see who could be the quietest on their horse. Equitation riding is all about how quiet the rider is on the horse and how well the horse performs, without being able to see the cue. Elbows in, heels down and a straight line from your shoulder to your heel. Dottie was great at this.

The first horse show came. Oh what fun! When they called my number I snapped to attention, ready to do my best for Dottie. Dottie smartly dressed was also ready and away we went. Around and around Walk, Trot, Walk, Trot, reverse and do it again. The judge looked at the smart little team and awarded us a ribbon. Little did we know everyone gets a ribbon in our division because we were so young and beginners. It encouraged us to do it again. Dottie learned to show me at halter for showmanship and rode me western pleasure. As she became older it was expected that we would not just walk and trot but also lope around the arena for judging. Getting a horse to lope takes a lot more coordination and cues. This was hard for Dottie with the leg braces. She mastered it but it was never easy for her. Her condition was corrected in a couple of years and the leg braces came off. She now had no problem giving me the cue to lope and did it well. We had passed the stage of everyone gets a ribbon to placing first through fifth. You had to be good to get a ribbon and even better to win the class. We were usually in the ribbons but seldom did we win the class, I was not a show pony and it showed. If Dottie was going to win in the shows, she needed a show horse like her mother rode.

Fort Rock

The show season was over by mid August except for the County Fair. The Arabian club always went on a weekend trail ride at a cattle ranch that one of the members owned. The ranch was in south central Oregon in the high desert. Next to the ranch was the historical monument of Fort Rock, where the Indian Captain Jack fought his last battle with the Calvary. Captain Jack was a renegade Indian that refused to go on a government reservation like the rest of the American Indian tribes had to do.

Fort Rock was this huge rock rising hundreds of feet above the desert floor, open on one side like a giant amphitheater. There were smaller out cropping of rocks inside the rock for the Indians to hide behind and take cover. The walls on the back side go straight up so no entrance from the rear unless you were a great rock climber. The battle was short as all the Calvary had to do was waiting for the Indians to run out of food and water. They could not get out of the rock enclosure and the Calvary could not get in.

The first ride was to the Devil's Gardens to see a herd of wild horses and have a picnic at the old homestead that was once a grand ranch. The Devil's Garden was a large valley surrounded by lava flows. These kept the wild horses from leaving the garden without any fences to keep them in. The horses would have to find a place where they could climb up onto the lava flow to find their way out. For this reason the horses were rounded up the day before and corralled so they would not see where we came into the garden.

As we rode across the lava flow you could see rings of lava rock stacked up a couple of rocks high. These were the last tell tale signs of the Indian encampments; they would pitch their teepee's on the lava flow for the warmth from the sun that the lava held all night. They would line the bottom of the teepee with rock to keep the wind from blowing under.

As we rode into the garden, Tiger started to dance and act peculiar, he being a stallion and two of his mares with him could smell the wild stallion's presence. Tiger was a very well mannered horse but he could not contain himself and started to whinny and beller. This echoed across the garden. He was letting the wild stallion know he was here and that he best keep his distance from Tiger's herd. It was not long until the wild stallion answered Tigers call and let him know we were on his turf. When we reached the ranch the two stallions saw each other through the coral fence but were never allowed to get close enough to challenge each other. Tiger finally settled down once he realized the wild one could not get to his mares.

Back at the ranch that night there was food and drink around the campfire at the main ranch house and lots of stories into the night. After some riders started for bed Dottie's mom and a few others decided to take a moonlight ride to the rock. Once there they noted one lone trailer in the camp ground with all the lights out. Knowing the story of Captain Jack they decided to act like Indians, swoop down and circle the trailer whooping and hollering like Indians, and then ride back to the ranch. Next morning when we looked towards the campground the trailer had left. We will never know if their leaving was planned or because they thought they were being haunted by the Indians of old. At best it was worth a good laugh.

The following day was a free day to explore a cave on the ranch where Sagebrush sandals from the A.D. era were discovered. That night a moon light ride was planned; 16 miles to Hole in the Ground and the ghost town of Freemont. Hole in the Ground is a huge crater where a meteor had hit the earth many centuries earlier. Freemont was an old frontier town where the stage coach stopped. There was a huge tree stump carved with steps that had been cut off just the right height for the stage coach so the ladies could get out easily. This was all that was left standing of the town and years later someone stole that. Now the town is seldom visited as no one can find it. Drinks and snacks were brought by jeep to the halfway point of the ride. On the way back the jeep would put flares along the road to mark the cattle guards and open the gates around them. Of course I managed to get Dottie's bag of Fritos before she could finish it. Dottie was too young for this long of a ride so would return to the ranch in the jeep with Granddad. She was not happy about this but settled down after granddad played with her a little. My saddle and bridle was put in the jeep and I was turned loose to follow the riders back to the ranch. Gypsy was ridden by Dottie's Grandmother, Muz by Dottie's father, and Tiger by Dottie's mom so I just fell in between them trotting along as I pleased in the dark. I would stop and nibble on the prairie grass and then trot real fast to catch up.

We were following old roads that had cattle guards in them to keep the cattle on each ranches range. These were large holes dug across the road then rail road iron put across leaving holes that the cattle's feet would fall into if they tried to cross. A truck could drive across these easily. Gates in the fence were on the side for moving the cattle around the cattle guards and these were marked with flares so no one would ride into them in the dark. An animal trying to cross one of these could break a leg or get their feet caught and not be able to get out. As we grew closer to the ranch the flares were burning lower and lower nearly going out as we approached. Not seeing any more flares and seeing the ranch lights some riders took off on a high gallop leaving the slower riders in the rear. I moved to the front of our horses with Gypsy right on my tail. All of a sudden we hear someone yell and a horse making terrible sounds. I stopped sharp alerting Gypsy something was wrong and the others stopped behind her. A flare had burned out and a rider in front of us had ridden into a cattle guard. He was lucky neither he nor his horse was hurt badly and we continued back to the ranch. Had I not stopped. Gypsy and grandmother would have been the next ones in the cattle guard. Grandmother had not ridden a horse in years and was no youngster. She would have been thrown and possibly badly hurt, not to mention my friend Gypsy. I saved the day or should I say night for our family. It was a celebration at the ranch with Fritos just for me.

I had great fun on this trip and loved the Oregon High Desert. It was a lifelong memory I would reflect back on too many times when I was old and gray. Dottie's grandparents lived in the high desert so I could only hope to return one day.

Lost

I did return to the Oregon high desert the following year when Dottie's mother and father went for a long weekend at grandmother's house. They took me along in the pickup canopy so Dottie and Art would have something to do while the adults were visiting. Plus they could ride me while Dottie's mother and grandmother walked to great grandmother's house across the way.

The area where they lived had dense Lodge Pole Pine trees and Buck Brush sandy soil an area where lots of city folks had summer homes and weekend cabins. Deer hunting and fishing was the past time when one was there. Dottie's great aunt and uncle also had cabins in this area so many family gathering went on here. Sometimes Dottie's mother and father would bring their horses and friends to trail ride while they visited the rest of the family.

Gypsy told me the story of one time when she and Tiger were riding with friends. Dottie was too small for her own horse so was riding behind her mother on Tiger. Tiger jumped over a rock and off went Dottie over his rump. Dottie's mom was quick to grab her ankle, swinging her upside down along side Tiger setting her in front of the saddle on his neck. This saved her from falling on the rock he had jumped over; she rode in the front of her mom the rest of the ride. This is a good lesson to always hold on when you are riding with someone else.

When we returned from great grandmother's house I was left in the yard with Dottie and Art. They were supposed to put me on the tether line before they went in for naps. Dottie tried to snap me up but the snap caught in the rope and did not close properly. After they went in the house the snap came off and I was loose in the yard. The yard gate had not been closed since I was supposed to be tied up.

Of course I went out the gate to see what else there was to see and eat. I started in the direction of great grandmother's house because I remembered a big bag of Fritos on the picnic table outside. I wandered for a while thinking I should have been there by now but could not find the house. I turned around to go back and realized I was lost with no idea which direction I had come from.

My wild instincts kicked in and I thought my best bet was to head for home, I mean home to Oregon City. I did not know that was 100 miles as I had ridden over in the pickup. My senses headed me west toward the Cascades Mountains, which I would have to cross to get home. I would also have to go north some 50 miles once I crossed the mountains to get home. As I wondered the woods were getting thicker the houses fewer and it was harder to see where I was going. The underbrush was now as high as all 39" of me so I had to stick to the old logging roads as much as possible. I hadn't seen a house in a while so I started to wonder where I would get a drink and something to eat.

Little did I know I had been missed and everyone was looking for me, in cars and on foot. Dottie's mom was tracking me but I had crossed the trail where they had taken me earlier so it was hard to figure out which way I had gone. They had called using CB radios and alerted everyone in the area to keep a sharp eye for a small red pony wandering around loose in the woods.

In the mean time I had stopped by someone's garden for a little snack only to be run off with a broom and some angry words. I continued on my merry way to the west until I came upon a large lake. It was directly in my path to the west and looked miles around. It had a huge dike on two sides with a road on the top. I went up onto the road where I could see boats of fishermen and a camp further down. My thoughts immediately turned to the Fritos I had originally started out for and headed for the camp.

Next thing I know pickups and jeeps are chasing me down the dike so I ran off into the woods, only to find people on foot chasing me also. They surrounded me until I had nowhere to run and just stopped. One man grabbed me by the halter and quickly put his belt through the ring so he had something to lead me with. I was taken down to the campground where I was tied to a tree. I was tired from all that chasing and was really scared. I didn't know any of these people, what were they going to do to me and where I would end up now. If only I had stayed in the yard I would not be in this mess.

To my relief I heard a familiar voice. It was Dottie's mom. She followed me on foot for miles through the trees. She had my bridle with her. She put it on over my halter, got on and away we went, back to the east and down the road. I had no idea how long it would take to get back to grandmothers house. It was getting dark and I was sure looking forward to that fenced yard, food, and people I knew. I would never leave Dottie again if we got back.

Things were even better when I saw the pickup pull up with Dottie and her dad in it. They loaded me in the back. Dottie sat with me and held my lead rope until we reached the house. There were no Fritos for my bad behavior but I didn't care as I was safe and with my family. Dottie's mom checked the rope and the snap and showed Dottie how to fasten it and how to check to make sure it was securely fastened. The next day after breakfast we headed for home. That was my last time in the high desert.

New Friend

Spring came and it was a year for babies. Dottie's mother did not breed the mares every year she liked to give them a good rest between raising babies. Gypsy had twins the year before but one was stillborn and it was too early to save the other one. For this reason she was bred back for this year. Usually only one mare was bred each year so there was always a horse to trail ride. Gypsy had twins again. It was great watching them run and play in the pasture. This is very rare for mares to have twins and not something breeders look forward to. They are a lot of work and usually one of them is a poor quality horse due to lack of nutrition. Mares are not well equipped to feed two foals.

Muz had a new foal at the same time so there would be no trail riding this year until the foals could be weaned. The babies are weaned at 5 or 6 months of age, depending on their physical attributes and need for the rich nutrition of their mother's milk over hay and grain with vitamins. Dottie's parents had a photographer friend that wanted to film a mare foaling. Muz was a quiet mare that has had several foals, so was a good choice to photograph. Muz was also very predictable when she would foal, eleven months and two days. She always waxed and dripped milk prior to foaling. These signs all gave plenty of time to set up the lighting and cameras. It was exciting to see all this going on in the arena barn in the middle of the night. Mares often foal in the night. This is a wild instinct so the foal has a chance to nurse and gather strength to run. Very few predators work at night so the foal would have many hours to gain strength before possibly encountering a predator looking to kill and eat it. Usually the mares foaled in a special foaling stall just for the occasion. This time Muz would be foaling in the indoor arena to allow room for the lights and everything. This also meant special attention would have to be given to the new foal to make sure it's eyes and nose were not filled with sand from the arena floor during the delivery. One of the 4-H kids had always wanted to see a mare foal so she was called to help with the delivery to make sure the foal was kept clean of sand until it jumped to its feet.

It was fun to watch the twins because everyday Muz's foal would invite one of them over for lunch. Muz would nip the visitor in the rump to shoe them away but they would go behind her and nurse between her legs where she could not reach them. Muz loved babies so she didn't fuss too much over the visitor or try to kick them. Gypsy was glad to get a break from feeding two babies all the time. Mares stay close to their new babies making sure they are safe and learn where the fences are, where the water trough is, and stuff like that. With twins, Gypsy could not do this because they never went together or in the same direction. It made her frantic trying to keep them safe. She was not equipped for this so she chose the smaller of the two as the one to take care of. She started to reject the larger foal and often would not allow her to eat when she wanted. Dottie's mother had kept a close watch on this situation and started bottle feeding the smaller foal early on, knowing Gypsy would not have enough milk for both of them. It was a blessing that Muz would allow the larger foal to eat with her foal on occasion. This helped make sure she got enough milk too.

Gypsy became ill one night. She was so sick that Dottie's mom called the vet to come and we were all worried. The babies were too small to lose their mother but the vet did not make it in time to save her. She had colic; rolling to relieve the pain she had twisted her intestine causing her death. Muz took the smallest twin and Dottie's mom bottle-fed the larger one. They did well and all three foals grew up happy and healthy. When they were old enough to wean I became the baby sitter. Well at least they were my size for a little while and I let them know I was the boss. They respected that even after they had grown larger than I and could easily have hurt me with a quick kick. They were too young to know they really had the advantage with their size but they did not have the confidence to try anything just yet.

Dottie's mother purchased a yearling colt Sharjurbay at the end of the show season last year. He was proving to be a great conformation horse. He was nicknamed Satan he was black as coal and full of mischief. Dottie's mom always showed the babies in conformation until their third year when they became old enough to start training. This taught them discipline, respect for humans, how to trailer and it was their first lessons in working to get into shape. They are worked 15 minutes a day at liberty trotting around to build leg strength and to muscle their loins. Satan had done well this spring in the shows and was proving to be a real contender. Black is a rare color for Arabians and many that are black do not have the best confirmation so not seen in the show ring often. Many breeders started breeding for color rather than confirmation, losing the best looking horses for black ones. He was one of two dark horses being shown that year so received a lot of attention for his color. At the first summer show, Satan caught a hind foot on the stall door jam and fell into the stall fracturing his Gaskin joint. We had no way of knowing if he would ever be sound or show again. Perhaps he would not be able to walk on that leg again. It was heart breaking for all of us to see him standing in the stall day and night on pain meds with the vets talking of putting him to sleep every time they came to check on him. Dottie's mom was just sick, especially after losing Gypsy just a couple of months prior to this. Satan did recover and became a wonderful sire, performance horse, and trail horse. All of us were relieved when he started walking on his leg again and Dottie's mother started conditioning him for training under saddle.

All this time Tiger was training hard for the National show, he had become a champion in several performance divisions. All who knew him were sure he would win a national title.

It was hard to think of Nationals but they were on our side of the country this year in Albuquerque, New Mexico. They rotated from East to West every other year making it less expensive to go. It was decided Tiger could do with a rest before the National show. He was qualified so did not need to show that much. He had to win so many classes to get qualified for Nationals but Tiger did not win a class, he was more like a machine than a horse. People that showed against him knew they were going to get second unless he made a mistake or something went wrong.

The family took the weekend off from showing for a class reunion. They had the neighbors come over to feed us while they were away. These neighbors were usually on time but this particular night they were having a party so showed up later than usual. Tiger became impatient for his dinner and started to chew on his wood gate. Livestock needs to be fed on a regular schedule. It keeps them from becoming anxious which causes them to lose weight. Everything seemed to be fine when they came to feed but the next morning Tiger was sick. The family was not due home until later that day. The neighbors called the vet but they were at a conference so an intern showed up instead. He thought Tiger just had Colic; a belly ache. He treated him with oil, told the neighbor to walk him, and left. Tiger became sicker as the day went on and the vet was called again. The family should be home soon. We were all hoping they would hurry but they had no idea anything was wrong. Again the intern showed up, gave him more oil, told them to continue walking him, and left.

The family arrived home and we were waiting for them to come to the barn. The neighbor was there walking Tiger, trying to keep him on his feet. His head was down on the floor with stuff running out of his nose. He could hardly stand, let alone walk. Horses like to roll up against something on their backs to relieve the pain in their stomach with colic. This can cause a twisted intestine like Gypsy had so you do not let them do this. You walk them trying to get the intestine to move the blockage through with the help of the oil to relieve the pain. Dottie's mother entered the barn and said, "Whose horse is that and what is wrong with him, was he hit by a car"? The neighbor said "no it's Tiger". He has been sick all day and we had the vet here twice, treating him for colic. Dottie's mother checked Tiger and said "this is no Colic" and called the vet again. When the intern answered, she said "get my vet on the phone or tell me where he can be reached, this horse is dying". The fluid running out of Tiger's nose was bad news for a horse; their throat is not designed like ours so they can not throw up like we do. This meant his stomach was so full when he put his head down that it ran back down his throat.

Our regular vet was reached and at the farm within the hour. It was decided that Tigers' stomach was blocked and they would need to do surgery to drain it and find out why. They covered the arena with sheets, laid Tiger down and performed surgery on his stomach. We were all quiet so as not to disturb Tiger with our noise and rustling around in the stalls. Thinking "Oh Good" Tiger is going to be OK. He has been saved. The surgery drained the stomach to find a piece of wood was blocking the intestine and it would have to be removed. This could not be done now as a horse can only be upside down for a short period of time before the weight of his stomach collapses his lungs. They must close surgery and let him up and go back in tomorrow for the stick. Tiger was much relieved and wanted to eat and drink. Water was all he could have for now and not much of that.

We awoke to Tiger really sick the next morning. The vet was called back again. Tiger lay down with his head on Dottie's moms lap. He had just stopped breathing when the vet arrived. Satan began to beller and act up in his stall, until Dottie's mother gave him a few good swats and told him to shut up. He has held his silence as long as he could he was letting us know he was now senior stallion at the ranch. Tiger was laid to rest with his long time friend Gypsy in the back pasture, under the giant Hemlock tree. This was the worst year of my life on the ranch, another friend gone. The only good news was the twins were doing well and Satan was getting stronger with every workout on his leg.

4-H Fun

One of the things I really enjoyed about this family was their interaction with the 4-H clubs and all the things they do. I was allowed to partake in the activities because Dottie's mom was the leader of what is today the oldest 4-H Horse Club in Clackamas County, Oregon.

There were all the kids and horses in the club of which eight made up the matched Chestnut Arabian Drill Team that participated in all the Parades around the area. Then there were a few members that showed their horse around the state at different breed and fun shows.

One of those I became good friends with because often Dottie's mom would take us to the show together. Dusty was his name and Shelly, was his owner. Dusty was a line back dun (Buckskin) Quarter Horse. Shelly also had an old pony called Cagey Caboose. He used to be Shelly's 4-H horse but now he was her younger sister Margo's horse. Margo was too young to show and Cagey (we think) had a heart attack or stroke the last time he was shown. It was a cold fall and there was only cold water for bathing. Cagey never seemed quite right after that bath. I never really got to know him because he passed away the next summer.

There was the Trail riding group, of which we all took one three day weekend every year for the whole club to go out as a thank you to the parents. The 4-Her's would do all the work on this weekend so their parents could relax and enjoy the outing. They did all the cooking, feeding and watering of stock, even saddled their parents horses for them, and cooled them out after the ride.

That was the best weekend of all. There were trail rides, obstacle courses to work over, long nights around the campfire telling stories, eating Fritos, and fishing along some lake or stream. That always turned into a swimming day for kids and horses that liked the water. Gypsy loved to swim and would go way out with Dottie's mother until just their heads could be seen above the water. I liked walking in the water but did not really take to swimming.

We were all tethered on a tie line stretched between trees with tie knots in it for each horse to be attached to. This was so we could not chew on the trees, which could kill them. Hay bags were hung from a higher line and we ate our grain out of nose bags that hung around our heads. It did not take long to learn not to throw your head to get the grain because it just flew out of the sack, up your nose and all over the ground. You had to put your head down on the ground so your nose could reach the bottom of the bag to get the grain.

We were led down to the stream for a drink before dark and we were bedded down for the night. Dottie's mom always made the last check to see that we were all tied up properly, our halters on just tight enough to not come off, yet loose enough to eat in. A bolin knot was tied around our necks with the rope that ran through the halter and tied to the tie line. This was just in case we did get the halter off so we were still tied up and had something around our necks to get a hold of if we did get off the line.

Dottie's mom had seen some horses get loose in the woods before. One did not come back for days. Another ran over a cliff and had to be put down. Others were lost and we never saw them again until the following year when someone else caught up to them, or they got hungry enough to come into someone else's camp for food, and were caught.

One year we were going to a new camp that had been donated to the 4-H foundation but needed work before being used. We went down a week ahead of the ride to fix tie stalls in this big old hay barn that had a floored area in the middle, for hay to be stored on. There were fishing lakes and lots of places to ride. I could not wait to go down for the ride, and I got to go on the work party trip to entertain Dottie and Art while their folks worked on the place, to get it ready.

When we all went down for the ride weekend, I was with Muz and Tiger and a great friend Frosty. This was his first trail ride. He belonged to one of Dottie's best friends Tanya and was a big quarter type gelding, whose color was kind of frosty looking for the color he was. All the kids bedded down in the middle of the barn on the wood floor. This put them head high with all of us horses. We were all tied in our separate stalls, fed hay and grain, given a water bucket, and bedded down for the night. It had been a long day and the kids were tired after dinner was cleaned up, so they all turned in early. Keep in mind this weekend was the 4-H'er's job to take care of everything for their parents. It was a long haul to this place and of course the kids had to explore everything before they started dinner and taking care of us.

Tanya was a short girl and Frosty was a really large horse for her. She often had trouble getting on him. He would not stand still and wait for her as well as he could have. She must have been having a dream or something, because soon after some of the girls went to sleep, Tanya began to talk in her sleep. Next thing we knew she got out of her sleeping bag and walked up to Frosty who was also sleeping, and easy to reach in this situation. Tanya doubled up her fist and hit Frosty smack in the nose, causing him to fly back against his rope and wake up the entire barn. Then she calmly walked back to her sleeping bag and went back to bed. Frosty was not hurt and everyone settled down after it happened.

The next morning everyone was talking about it and laughing at how funny it was. Tanya did not remember a thing and thought everyone was making it up to play a trick on her. It took a long time to convince her she had really hit Frosty. When she walked over to pat him, he backed up and looked at her wide eyed. That proved something of what they were saying must have happened because he was not acting like that when someone else walked up to him.

This whole weekend had its funny parts. There was bass in one of the lakes and Dottie's mom caught enough for everyone the last day we were there. They did not have time to eat them, so took them home for a meal later on. One family that was new to the club, and not from the Pacific Northwest, offered to have a party at their place the following weekend and cook the fish.

When we all arrived, the fish were on the grill and smelled divine. We played horse games and had a lesson while the dinner was finished. When everyone sat down to eat, Dottie's mom took a bit of her fish and got a real funny look on her face. The fish were really crunchy. You could hear it when they were chewing. Dottie's mom said "John, did you scale these fish before you cooked them?" John not being from this part of the country had never seen a bass, let alone cooked one. He had no idea that they had scales or that they needed to come off before you cooked them. Everyone laughed, began skinning their fish, and finished the meal.

Another time when everyone was telling stories around the campfire, one mother told how great her father was with their pets. He would go to the auction and buy calves to raise for meat for the family and when the calves were ready to butcher, he would take them back to the auction. He would sell their friends and buy other calves to butcher, so they would not have to eat their friends. As she told the story, she realized that all those years they had been eating their friends. It was just a story their father told them so they would not feel so bad about it. She began to cry and then broke out into a loud laugh at how gullible she had been all those years thinking he fed these animals to eat, and then sold them to someone else for the kids' sake.

One of Dottie's mom's stories was about side hill cows. She always got the kids with this one and it usually took them days to figure out it was a joke. She would talk about the trails around the hills where the cattle were grazed all summer around the hill. Then in the winter they were brought to the barn and fed hay. There was a trough in the middle of the barn for the water to run out when they washed down the cement. She would tell the kids it was there so the cows would not tip over in the winter because they had two short legs and two long legs, so they would not fall off the hill. In the winter they would walk with their two long legs in the trough and their short legs on the cement so they would not tip over in the barn. Oh what a laugh this would bring when they figured it out. I so remember riding along and hearing her say "there are some side hill cows up there", with the straightest face in all serious tones. All the great memory of those special years with the 4-H'ers has given me years of enjoyment recalling stories like these.

One year we had so many kids in the club and many without horse trailers or trucks. Dottie's mom bought a new bigger truck so she could haul more horses to the shows. We had so many going camping this year that there was no room for me in the truck. I thought I was going to get left home. What a disaster because this is always my biggest weekend of the year to score Fritos. I see Dottie's dad putting together a couple of 2x6's. Then he nailed 2x4's across them like a ladder. I wondered what that was for as we never needed a ladder in the woods before. I saw him lay it up against the truck just below the tack room door and start measuring on it again for something else. He came back with a couple of pipe fittings from his plumbing truck and a couple of bent pieces of pipe. He started attaching the pipe to the ladder and laid it back up against the truck tack room door. Now I saw that the pipe holds the ladder to the door opening so you can walk up to put your stuff in the tack room. Pretty slick I thought as the truck was really high off the ground and you always needed someone to hand stuff up to you, in order to load it.

I still could not figure out why the cross pieces because it was going to be hard for people to step over those with an arm load of tack. Well he seemed to be pleased with it. He asked Dottie's mother what she thought and she said, "Well let's try it".

She headed to the barn and the next thing I knew she was headed in my direction with a halter and lead rope. Now I was really puzzled. What do I have to do with this contraption? She caught me and led me out to the truck; the ramp was not down so what did she expect me to do?

She started up the ladder and gave me a little pull. What was I thinking? Oh I see. It is a ramp for me to get into the tack room so I can go on the trail ride. I am pretty good at loading but this was really steep and narrow, a wrong step and I could fall off.

When you want a horse to do something out of the ordinary, you need to show confidence to them that you believe they can do it. Then you need to support their effort to get it done. That is exactly what happened. I started up the ramp slowly with Dottie's mom supporting my head and her dad standing at my side on the ground, to see that I didn't fall off. Up was pretty easy but down was a little more of a challenge. I made it with their help. Dottie's mom went out of the truck and had me wait until she was on the ground beside the ramp. Dottie's dad was on the other side to steady me on the way down. I would do anything to get to go on the ride, even though it was a little scary. I was determined to make it work as it was my ticket to the ride.

A really great thing the 4-H club would do is donate six weeks of their time to work with physically and mentally challenged people. I always got to go on this one. We did it one night a week. The bus would arrive at Clackamas County Fairgrounds where we were waiting. Each person on the bus was assigned a horse and a team to help them with their horse. All types of people with different disabilities had the chance to ride for six weeks. There would be little show events, costume classes, and at the end there was a horse show with trophies and ribbons for all. It was amazing to see how this time with us horses changed their lives in such a short time. We hated to say goodbye but looked forward to seeing them next year.

One little rider named Alex drew Muz for his horse. He did not talk and he would wet his pants. By the end of the six weeks Alex could say "that's my horse" and he would let us know when he needed to go to the bathroom so he didn't wet his pants. People could not believe it the first time they heard him talk, little did they know he had been talking to us horses from the first night.

The Leader

We had the big truck that would haul five head of horses. The 4-H'er's without trailers rode with Tiger or Satan and Muz in our truck. When it was full I rode in the tack room in front of the horse compartment. It was a little crowded when there was camping equipment and saddles in there.

I remember one time when there was just enough room for me in the back of the truck, Dottie's dad loaded me last, and closed up the truck. I am very good at getting loose as I love to chew on ropes to pass the time. It was not long until the truck stopped and the ramp opened to see what was going on back there. The horses where moving a lot more than usual and Dottie's mom knew something was not right when that was happening. Well it was me. I got my rope untied and decided to walk under everyone to the front to bother Satan. He was not near as tolerant of me as Tiger had been, so it was fun to get to him when I knew he couldn't get to me.

Bad thing was we had to find a spot to get off the road, unload everyone but Satan, and reload the truck. This time Dottie's mom tied me up to make sure I would not get loose again. Dottie's dad did not do this stuff enough to be good at it like her mom was, making it easy for me to get loose.

Satan never did like me but he did put up with me when he had too.

With spring came the shows with short trail rides in between for Satan to learn about the woods, creeks and bridges. He was now the leader and Dottie's moms' horse for everything like Tiger used to be. He had to learn all about the parades, trail riding, as well as being a show horse. Trail riding would give him a rest from the show ring stress. The 4-H club was staying at the horse camp at Timothy Lake on Mt Hood for their big riding weekend this year. Their first ride was a short one for lunch at Little Crater Lake. This was a new trail no one had been on before, so we took it easy and watched for anything out of the ordinary. I fell into line right behind Satan who was following one of the 4-H'er's horses down the trail through the woods. because he had never led a ride. Dottie was quite experienced from our last two years, so very comfortable now and able to ride all day with the rest of the group.

The first thing we encountered was bees on the trail, they burrow in the ground and after the first few horses walked over the hive, they were mad and looking for someone to sting. They started on the bellies of the last couple of horses in the line. Thank goodness they were old seasoned trail horses and their riders were the parents who knew what to do. The horses wanted to buck and run but we always took insect spray with us for such occasions and as soon as they started spraying the bees, they left. We marked the trees so we would ride around the nest on the way back, to avoid this from happening again.

We came into a clearing with a long boardwalk with no sides for horses. It crossed a large marsh area that was too wet to cross any other way. There was no trail for horses to go around and the boardwalk was built plenty strong and wide for horses. It did have a slip rail on it so a horse's foot would not slide off the edge, if the wood was wet. We could not see how long this was or where it came out. The lead mare started down the boardwalk with Satan on her heels, when they came to a sharp corner. The mare did not turn the corner. She became confused and jumped off the bridge into the marsh. Satan not knowing what to do, stopped as the mare floundered around in the mud and water, trying to keep her feet. Her rider was able to get off and get back on the boardwalk, but there was no way to get the horse back onto the walk. The mare would have to follow along in the marsh until we reached dry land. We checked to see that the mare was not injured before continuing onto the lake for lunch. As we had lunch we talked of how we were going to get back. We did not want to take the road as it was busy with cars as well as log trucks. We needed to figure out how to keep all the horses on the walk if we were going to return the way we came. We definitely needed a different lead horse that we knew would go around the corner without stopping or jumping off. Satan led the rest of the way across but he had someone walking in front of him. Would he lead the way back? We had no way of knowing but it was worth a try. After all, Dottie's mom was the most experienced rider, so the most likely to keep him going and on the walk.

Satan took off in the lead after lunch and was doing fine through the trees and the brush. I was right on his heels with Dottie and everyone else in behind us. Upon seeing the boardwalk, Satan stopped dead. I came to the rescue walking around him and onto the boardwalk. I took care to see that Dottie was OK with us leading, then looked back at Satan and said "come on, it's OK". Satan fell right into line with his nose on my rump and across we went. All 18 horses made it across and around the corner without incident. Now Satan moved back into the lead and we just had to watch for the bees in the trail. It wasn't long until we saw our marks and ties in the trees that showed us where we had encountered them before. Satan was turned out into the brush to make a new trail around the nest. He did this well, with no worries. We were back on the trail shortly thereafter and headed for camp.

Some of the kids wanted to do more riding, but Dottie was tired so we did not go. It wasn't long until we heard a horse come running and kids yelling something about bears. Dottie's mom was up in a flash to see what the commotion was about. The kids had come upon some baby bears and some of them were trying to chase them. Dottie's mom told the others to go back and get these children out of there before the mother bear came back. That would have been really bad, not to mention how scared the little bears must have been with the horses and humans all around them.

Everyone went back to camp where there was a lesson on bears and what not to do when you see them. We talked about our experience with the bridge and the bees, and then it was time for fun and dinner around the camp fire. Hurray, it was a celebration around the campfire that night and I was the guest of honor for leading everyone across the bridge. Yes, you guessed it. I was snatching Fritos as fast as anyone sat their stash down where I could reach it.

One of the nice things about being small and dependable is that you only get hooked to the tie line when everyone is going to bed. The rest of time I was loose to snoop and graze where I pleased, as long as I did not leave our camp. If I went to someone else's camp on the line, I went with everyone else.

A Girl Friend

All this time I was having a great life, but I never had anyone my own size to run around with. It gets old keeping out of the big horse's way and looking up at everyone all the time. It is hard on the neck and back, and as I got older, I found I was not as quick at moving out of the way as I used to be. They didn't mean to hurt me, but sometimes I was just in the wrong place at the wrong time.

For a brief period of time there was another pony in the barn, but she was not allowed out to play. She was a champion show pony so she was kept in the stall with long feet and big shoes with pads. She was not allowed out because she might break a hoof if she was allowed to run on those long feet. Not to mention she might injure a leg with the weight of the shoes and pads.

These were part of being a show pony, to help you pick up your front feet really high and be stylish. Her mane was really long so that it could be braided with ribbons at the show, and her tail had to be braided up all the time to keep it from breaking off. The show ponies have long flowing tails that drag along the ground behind them.

The bottom line was that I was just a horse compared to her and I was not allowed around her. She was moved to a show stable a few months later and I never saw her again.

Dottie had a few lessons on how to show her but never got to go to a show with her, before she left. The trailer left one day shortly after the show pony left, and returned later with a new pony. She was a dapple gray, just my size, and she was fine.

Come to find out she was going to be a show pony for Dottie but she was allowed to go out with me in the pasture. I liked her a lot. Her registered name was Flashy Lassie, and she was a real looker, a beautiful dapple gray with long flowing mane and tail. Once we became acquainted it was my job to show her around and introduce her to the rest of the horses. She had been a yard pet for some older folks that could no longer keep her. They allowed her to get overweight and out of shape.

It was Dottie's job to work Lassie and get her into shape to show. Her feet were shod so they would grow long and her tail was braided up. Her training began. First she had to learn to load in the trailer. This is where I came in. I would walk into the trailer and wait for her to join me, and then we would go for a little ride together and come back to the pasture.

Once she had the loading and hauling down, it was time to teach her to stand properly for a judge to look at her. She had to learn to trot around the arena next to Dottie, then stop and stand at attention in a stretch. She must hold this position as long as it takes, depending on how many ponies there are to be judged before her in the class. That could be from five to 15 minutes. She had to walk up and pose for the judge and then trot off, showing her high knee action and beautiful flowing movement.

Dottie had to learn how to braid Lassie's mane with ribbons and put in the flags (cut pieces of ribbon) to decorate the mane ribbons. This is true for many breeds to be braided with long flowing ribbons to decorate their manes and forelocks. Each breed has its own design for the ribbon flags and the placement of the ribbons.

Lassie and I shared a big stall and had our own pasture. It was great having someone to share my life with. She liked to lie in the grass sunning for the warmth it provided in the morning. I loved lying near her and relaxing in the warmth, watching to see what she would do next.

After a few shows it was time for Lassie to learn to be ridden. She had never experienced a saddle or anything on her back except a blanket. It is hard to train us because we are too small for adults to ride. This makes our training twice as hard and takes twice as long. We must be driven to learn how to go and which way to turn when there is pressure on the side of our mouth. We carry sacks of something to resemble a child's weight until it is safe to put a child on us. It was all new and strange for Lassie and she was frightened and wanted to fight the tight cinch and iron bit. I talked to her and let her know if she went along with it, she would not be hurt and it could really be fun.

They would saddle Lassie up and have Dottie ride me and lead her. They would load a grain bag on her back to simulate a person's weight. You must be very careful with ponies not to overload them even though they are capable of carrying twice their weight. The origin of the pony in the work force was to carry heavy loads of ore out of the mines. We are small and can fit down the same shafts as a man, so became the workhorse of the miners that pulled the ore carts down the rails out of the shafts. We worked alongside the small burros in the western mining camps.

Lassie was finally ready for Dottie to ride and her mother would lead her around the arena gradually letting the lead get longer and longer. This allowed Dottie to steer

Lassie with her hands and push her with her legs in different directions so she learned to go where her rider wanted her too. After a few rides, Dottie's mom took her and Lassie outside to the big arena with no line. Dottie would make Lassie go around and turn her different directions at the walk, until she was good at that. Then Dottie asked Lassie to trot by squeezing her with her legs and making clicking noises with her mouth to encourage Lassie to go forward. Lassie learned pretty quickly and was soon doing well at being a saddle horse.

It was now time to go on a trail ride with Satan to lead the way. They loaded up in the truck. I told her to just follow Satan and she would be OK. They were gone for a long time and I began to worry that something had gone wrong. When they returned I was anxious to find out how it went. Lassie said it was fine until they came to a bridge. She was afraid to cross the bridge and tried to turn around and go back to the truck. Dottie's mom put a rope on her bit and led her behind Satan across the bridge and down the trail a little way. Then she took the rope off and they continued to ride down the trail a little further. On the way back Lassie just stayed close to Satan and followed Satan across the bride and back to the truck. She had a good time but would have liked it better if I could have gone too. I said maybe someday when Dottie's little brother Art started riding, we could go together. Art never did ride much. He just did not enjoy the horses like the rest of the family did.

Lassie was taken out to one show and she and Dottie did great. They came home with a big ribbon and Lassie had many stories to tell about that day. She met a new family at the show that really liked her. Their little girl was in love.

It was not long before the family came to visit and played with Lassie and rode her around the arena for a while. Their little girl was ready for her first horse and Lassie was to be that horse. They came several more times and took lessons from Dottie's mom, and then they came with a trailer and took Lassie home with them. I never saw her again.

I wasn't totally without a friend my own size because Dottie's mom had purchased a larger pony for Art, hoping he would ride. This pony's name was "Honeybee" and she was one of those ponies people say bad things about. She had been mistreated so she took it upon herself to mistreat Art every time she got a chance. One day she pushed him down with her nose and walked right up his back. He wasn't hurt but sure could have been. I tried to tell her this home was different, but she had been mistreated one too many times to believe it. Dottie's mom could not take the chance Art would get hurt, so Honeybee was sold at the auction. This only happened when Dottie's mom could not look someone in the eye and guarantee them a horse was safe for them or their child. Auctions have signs all over saying "let the buyer beware" everything sold as is!

You can try a horse at the auction and you can talk to the owner but you never know if they are telling you the truth or not. Dottie's mom did not stay at the auction because she did not want to talk to people about Honeybee. She would not lie, so she just dropped her off and left.

The Parade

We had been to the horse shows trail riding, and now it was parade time. I liked to pull the cart and it would be Art's first ride away from home. I had lots of experience in parades so it was nothing new to me. I just follow whatever is in front of me and walk down the white line. Stay in the middle of the street and stop when the parade stops and start when it starts moving again. Turn the corners real wide so not to hit anyone on the curb and keep a sharp eye for children running out to pet me. Make sure I do not step on their feet or run over them with the cart wheels. Dottie's mother walked on the side just in case Dottie needed a little assistance but I took charge and no help was needed. After the parade I waited patiently for the prizes to be handed out, I won a big trophy for my young drivers that day. Art never became involved with the horses like Dottie but he did grow up to love, own and drive the big draft horses in parades and weddings in the Seattle area for a couple of years.

I spent many years with Dottie before once again being outgrown. She had grown into Muz and was riding her at all the shows. Then one Christmas she put a Pinto on her list for Santa. Back then Arabians were not shown if they had spots. It was highly frowned on to have a white spot or stocking above the knee. There was always a lot of effort to accommodate Dottie's Christmas list because she was born on Christmas day. Why did she want a pinto with 16 head of beautiful Arabians to choose from? Well Pintos are very popular with the young girls and that is what Dottie wanted for Christmas. There were two occasions to celebrate for her and no one was allowed to give one gift for both occasions. Christmas Eve was always celebrated for Christmas and Christmas Day was always a birthday bash.

Dottie's mom had been training a half Arabian daughter of Satan's that was bright red with white spots. Her name was Marati and she was trained to ride and drive. The couple that owned her was great friends with Dottie's parents so agreed to lease Marati to Dottie for the show season. Depending on how that went, they might consider selling her to Dottie when the season was over.

Christmas was special at our house, Christmas Eve after we were fed there were eight little piles of hay placed around the indoor arena and the big arena door was left open. This was so Santa could fly in and the reindeer could have a snack while he left the presents for Dottie and Art. Then when midnight came Dottie's dad would run around outside the house with some sleigh bells while Dottie's mom would wake up the kids. They would hurry to the window to see Santa and Rudolph fly away, but of course they never did see them. They only heard the sleigh bells. The next morning they would hurry to the barn to see if the reindeer ate the hay. They never noticed the horse tracks around where the pile had been it was Muz that ate the hay.

When Christmas came there was a big stuffed spotted horse under the tree. Everyone could see the disappointment in Dottie's face. There was a big tag attached to the stuffed horse. As Dottie read the note she began to jump up and down. The note said "Merry Christmas from Santa now go to the barn and you will see the horse that would not fit under this tree".

Dottie could not get dressed fast enough. She ran to the barn and there was her pinto horse that she had asked for. The season went well. There were many ribbons and trophies, but it was just a walk-trot show season. Dottie was taking lessons trying to learn how to lope Marati, but her legs were too short to cue her right and Marati was too green to pick it up on her own.

Dottie decided Muz was the horse for her because she was fully trained and would lope when the announcer called for it. Muz knew everything and made it very easy for Dottie to win with little effort on her part. Years later she would graduate to ride Muz's son Seynrif, a park horse, and become the accomplished English rider she is today. She rode western but never favored it like her mother does.

My Last Home

I had virtually been retired. There was no one in this family or in the neighborhood for that matter that needed a pony. I had become a yard ornament, a lawn mower for places that were hard to get too. I was loved and cared for as usual but with nothing to do, I became fat and lazy.

Dottie's mom ran into a family at the auction looking for a safe pony for their children to play around and learn to take care of, maybe a little riding from time to time in the yard.

I was sold for the last time to this home with many little riders eager to learn about a horse. They became good friends of Dottie's mother so I was visited often for many years. I remembered what Dottie's mother always said when my friends were sold, "you can always come back".

I never had to come back. This family was great and often called on Dottie's mother for advice to make sure I had everything I needed for my age. The children all grew up with a healthy love and respect for horses, never encountering that mean little pony so many often speak of in their life, that drove them away from horses. Several of the children continued with horses throughout their lives and their children learned about horses as well, for which I was the example.

I lived well into my thirties, with never a cruel hand, or a missed meal. This is the life every horse deserves and with it will come many years of loyal, loving service to the people who care for us. Notice that I said care for not own. In today's world with proper training, a horse has a mutual agreement to work for humans. Unlike the old days when horses were broke to work, which often meant breaking our spirit and making us numb to feelings, so we would just obey. In those days we were nothing more than an animal needed to get something done, unlike today, where we are pets to be enjoyed, loved, and be a part of the family.

Glossary

Bolin   This is a knot that never can be pulled so tight it cannot be untied nor will it slip and become tighter. Excellent for livestock as they can become scared and pull to get away. Because of their size and weight this can pull a knot so tight the rope then has to be cut away or cause slipping that can choke the animal.

Cattle   These are used in large areas of land (thousands of acres) on

Guards   roads to keep cattle from crossing into other areas. They are the width of the road and 4 to 6 feet in length, to prevent animals from stepping over them. They are a hole dug in the ground then crisscrossed with rails so you can drive across them but animals cannot walk or jump across them. Most animals will step into the first hole and pull their leg out, and not attempt to cross any further.

Clipped   This is a term used when a horse gets a haircut. The bridle path is clipped so the halter and bridle can be buckled without getting caught in the mane. The nose whiskers are shaved off and the hair under the jaw to make their heads cleaner to look at. Their ears are shaved out in the summer just for a cleaner look. The hair is left on in the winter to keep them warm. If they are living in an area with lots of bugs it is best to leave some hair in the ears, to keep the bugs out.

Colic   When a horse gets a stomachache due to bad feed or worms. They cannot have a bowel movement (impaction) and often try to roll up on their backs to relieve the pain. They may roll up against a wall or fence to help keep them upside down. This is often referred to as being cast up against a wall. This may result in death by causing an intestine to twist or due to impaired lung function for breathing. A horse's lungs are up against their back bone. Their stomach is below the lungs, making it very hard to breathe when lying on their back. A vet pumps oil into a horse's stomach to move through the intestine and relieve the impaction. Often times just walking a horse will help get the intestines moving again. It is critical that a horse not be allowed to roll violently or become cast when coliced.

Cool   Down A horse should never be allowed to drink large amounts of water at one time when very hot or over heated. A horse should never have cold water run on his back when he is over heated. Both of these can cause colic, cramping in the back and loin muscles. This can result in severe pain and possible death for a horse. A horse should be walked out to cool down if very hot or sponged off with luke warm water and tied up to cool down slowly. A blanket or cooler may be used to cover the horse absorbing the moisture from their coat as they cool down also blocking air that is too cold allowing them to cool down slowly.

Conformation   Each breed of horse has a distinct look and way of going that makes each breed different from one another. The different characteristics of the body are known as the conformation of the horse; size, build, way of going and overall look.

Cue   This is the term used to give a horse a command with your leg, your hands, or verbally. It tells the horse what you want them to do and the direction you want them to move. This cue should be barely detectable by the human eye. It can be as slight as a touch of the calf of the leg or a raise of the hand to signal the horse to do something different. Verbal cues are also used in the training of horses. It is important that the words are very distinctive and cannot be confused with another word used for something else. Cue words should be one word as animals do better with one word rather than a lot of words or a sentence.

Dike
: An earth dam made to hold back or control water flow.

Drive
: We speak of driving a horse anytime we are working behind or beside the horse using long lines. He may be hitched to something he is pulling or may be driven by walking with long lines to direct the horse. One needs to make sure if they are driving from behind they stay well out of reach should the horse kick.

Equitation
: This refers to how the rider looks on the horse. Do they sit properly, are they quiet with their hands, and is their body quiet as the horse moves under them.

Float
: This refers to horses teeth needing to be seen by the dentist. It is done with a large file and power tools much like you experience when you go to the dentist. Their mouth should be checked regularly (every other year) for points that stop them from chewing their food properly. This may need to be done yearly after a horse reaches the age of 15 years and more.

Gait
: This term refers to the different ways a horse moves. Example: walk, trot, gallop (lope), pace, single foot, canter, running walk, rack.

Gaskin
: The first joint on the hind leg of a horse, below the hip.

Green   This is a term used when a horse is started under saddle for 30 to 60 days. Often referred to as Green broke, meaning they have been ridden and had some work but need to be finished. These are not dependable for beginners unless they are going to get more training for themselves and the horse.

Intern   Like a doctor, a veterinarian must study under a licensed veterinarian after school, before practicing as a vet. During this period they are referred to as an intern.

Lava Flow This refers to rock formations formed by the hot molten lava that flowed from ancient volcanoes across the high desert.

Liberty   This refers to working a horse loose in a round pen or small arena. It is a time for them to learn voice commands and to strengthen their legs and back. It can be used to condition halter horses, as well as start saddle training.

Lunge   This term is used when working a horse on a 30' line in a circle. It also can be used when conditioning or training a horse. One should seek training on how to work a horse from the ground regardless of which method you decide to use.

Reverse   A term used meaning to change direction in a show ring or training ring during a lesson, riding class, liberty or lunge work.

Slaughter   For many years it was acceptable to kill horses for meat, both for human and animal consumption. Horses that were dangerous to humans, old or sick, were often sent to slaughter. Wild horses were rounded up and slaughtered for money. This is no longer the practice in the United States but it is still acceptable in many foreign countries

Sound   We refer to soundness of a horse when we are talking about his legs and joints. Is he lame (does he limp?) Are his feet, legs and joints correct?

Tether   This is to tie or stake a horse on a long line (30 feet) so they can eat but not leave. It may be attached to a tree or a stake in the ground. A horse must be taught how to do this or they can become tangled in the rope and throw themselves to the ground. This can cause an injury to the legs like a rope burn or worse.

Warm up   A horse is like any athlete that needs to stretch and warm up their muscles before going to work. This is accomplished by walking, turning and slow trotting, before beginning a hard regiment of work. Unlike the movies, a horse should never be gotten on and rode off in a hard gallop or run from a standing position. without being warmed up.

www.ingramcontent.com/pod-product-compliance
Lightning Source LLC
Chambersburg PA
CBHW021255280526
45784CB00005B/2388